Cover Story

On Saturday, September 2, 1961, before a crowd of 14,106 racing fans at Fort Erie Race Track, a strapping bay colt named Puss n Boots wrote his name into Canadian racing lore when he dumped his rider and plunged into one of the track's infield lakes.

See page 40 for more on this scoundrel.

Dedicated to Horsemen Everywhere

To the: Grooms
Exercise Riders
Pony Boys
Hotwalkers
Jockeys
Valets
Trainers
Jockey's Agents
Veterinarians
Blacksmiths
Starting Gate Crew

…all those who collectively are responsible for the
daily care and well-being of the real stars…the plucky steeds
who compete with grit and courage on our nation's race courses.

ballads of the turf
...and other doggerels

by william galvin

with short stories by

Jim Coleman

For Doug
Good Luck in the
2009 Puss n Boots Cup

Bill Galvin

PUBLISHER: WILLIAM GALVIN
EDITOR: AMY HARRIS
LAYOUT AND DESIGN: SARAH TAYLOR
TECHNICAL ASSISTANT: TAMARA GREEG
COMPOSITION: HONG XIAO

ILLUSTRATIONS BY:
DIANNE HORTON BARNSLEY
ELAINE MACPHERSON
KIT MO
JOHN VERDURA

PERMISSIONS:
THE TORONTO GLOBE AND MAIL
THOROUGHBRED RACING ASSOCIATIONS (TRA)
CANADIAN HORSE PUBLICATIONS
MICHAEL BURNS
ELAINE MACPHERSON

Library and Archives Canada Cataloguing in Publication

Galvin, William J., 1931-
Ballads of the turf and other doggerels / William J. Galvin ;
illustrators,
Elaine Macpherson ... [et al.].

Poems.
ISBN 0-9781370-0-0

1. Horse racing--Poetry. 2. Horsemen and horsewomen--Poetry. I.
Title.

PS8613.A4599B35 2006   C811'.6
C2006-904443-0

PRINTED AND BOUND IN CANADA

VISIT THE AUTHOR AT WGALVIN@TREBNET.COM

Contents

Chatahoochee Smith

by Jim Coleman

Forty years ago, a good Samaritan motorist braked his car to a stop when he saw a small truck stuck hopelessly in the deep mud on the shoulder of the old No. One highway between Regina and Winnipeg.

The motorist got out of his car, walked across the highway and peered inside the truck. There were no apparent casualties, but the truck contained a peculiar cargo. There was one grizzled man sitting in the front seat, singing to himself as he awaited rescue. In the back were two Thoroughbred racehorses and a barber chair. The horses, one of which was sprawled over the barber chair, had expressions of resignation on their careworn faces.

The driver of the mired truck was Chatahoochee Smith, the gypsy horseman who, when spring came each year, closed his little barbershop on Eighth Avenue in Calgary and went away to the races. One of the horses in the back of the truck was Chatahoochee, the old chestnut mare from whom Smith acquired his racetrack nickname. The other was a nondescript pelter whom Smith acquired for $300.

A Great Talker

That was the way Chatahoochee Smith travelled in the Depression years: two horses and a barber chair in the back of the truck as he drove from track to track. When the horses were bedded down in their stalls at each track, Chatahoochee put his barber chair in a sunny spot at the end of the shedrow, and with fellow horsemen as his customers, he practiced his tonsorial profession to acquire sustenance for himself and his noble beasts.

Chatahoochee finally died, just two days ago, in a Calgary nursing home at the age of 82. He was one of the last of the truly colourful western horsemen. Chatahoochee has gone on to his final reward, but his name is certain to live on in the picturesque legends of the west.

He was born in Dundas, Ontario and was christened Walter Edward Smith, but for some obscure reason of his own, he always signed documents as Jack Smith. One of his sisters, who was residing in Toronto until a couple of years ago, was a teacher of elocution. His sister's vocation probably explains Chatahoochee's histrionic ability. He became a national celebrity in 1964 when he appeared in a beautiful film, Woody's Wish, which Michael Magee produced for CBC. Chatahoochee co-starred with a horse named Woody's Wish and, in the final scene, the old horseman was sitting in a tackroom, reciting a racetrack poem entitled 'The Ballad of Chatahoochee Smith.'

Actually, the poem was written by Bill Galvin of the Ontario Jockey Club, but with the harmless imaginings of old age, Chatahoochee ultimately managed to convince himself that he, personally, was the author of the ballad.

Western horsemen seldom were given stabling accommodation at Toronto's old Woodbine in the 1930s. But, on the urging of Jim Speers of Winnipeg, Major Palmer Wright, the punctilious secretary of the Ontario Jockey Club, once agreed to provide stalls at Woodbine for four horses trained by Chatahoochee Smith.

Little knowing what was in store for him, Major Wright retired to sleep in his private bedroom in the directors' building at Woodbine on the night when Chatahoochee arrived from the west.

After the horses had been unloaded and placed in their Woodbine stalls, Chatahoochee examined his surroundings. It was a moonlit night and, as he stared across the track, he could see all that lush green grass in the Woodbine infield.

That's Holy Ground

Many months had passed since Chatahoochee's horses had seen green grass. He decided they needed an immediate change of diet. One by one, he led his four horses across the track and turned them loose to gambol on the greensward of the infield. Little did he know he was trespassing on holy ground – he was permitting his shaggy Cayuses to romp on Woodbine's carefully manicured steeplechase course, which was Major Wright's particular pride and joy.

The Major was awakened at the crack of dawn by a distraught watchman banging on his bedroom door. While the watchman babbled and pointed to the infield, The Major peered through his bedroom window. Major Wright almost burst a blood vessel when he saw Chatahoochee's scruffy animals desecrating his beloved steeplechase course.

Never again was Chatahoochee Smith granted stable accommodation at Woodbine.

The little barbershop on Calgary's Eighth Avenue has long since disappeared. The hair clippers, the scissors and the old straight-edged razors had been retired permanently before they persuaded him to enter that Calgary nursing home. No man ever was destined to stay among us forever and now Chatahoochee Smith has gone to a faster track.

April 25, 1972

Reprinted with permission from The Globe and Mail

Illustration by Elaine Macpherson

'Twas a sight to behold as that half-ton rolled with its cargo of quaint attire
For the ramp and pails and sundry things were fastened with bailing wire.
Twixt the colt and mare, was the barber's chair (with the dual occupation),
And thus they came to the Stampede Grounds, midst that annual jubilation.

The Ballad of Chatahoochee Smith

This is a tale that was told to me by a gyp with snow-white hair,
In a shakedown bed, right under the shed of Big Jim Fair.
The waves of Lake Ontario could be heard as they lashed the shore,
As he spun this yarn, 'neath the old frame barn, inside the feedroom door.

This man who'd fought the demon rum, recalled when he made his mark,
For he'd travelled the bull rings to Juarez and the milers to Belmont Park.
The saga he told began to unfold, it's following herewith,
The unbelievable doggerel of Chatahoochee Smith.

He told of a Calgary barber, who worked at his trade until
Given that Chatahoochee mare by a gent called Basso Bill.
He picked up another two-year-old, out where Chinook winds blow,
Then with colt and mare and barber chair, to the Stampede Grounds did go.

'Tis said that prairie wheatlands ripened prematurely on the day
When Chatahoochee loaded up the chestnut and the bay.
And the bowels of the earth, to oil beds gave birth, thus went the old man's ditty,
When that derelict truck (with plenty of luck), made it to Calgary City.

The Ballad of Chatahoochee Smith

'Twas a sight to behold as that half-ton rolled with its cargo of quaint attire
For the ramp and pails and sundry things were fastened with bailing wire.
Twixt the colt and mare, was the barber's chair (with the dual occupation),
And thus they came to the Stampede Grounds, midst that annual jubilation.

At the loading dock, he removed his stock and the populace looked aghast,
As he said, "vamoose" and turned 'em loose to fare on prairie grass.
He sought his stalls mid jeering calls of those who thought him daft,
Then set up store near the feedroom door while everybody laughed.

His barber's trade was one that paid for they came from miles around
For a trim and shave by this fearless knave who'd shipped to Calgary town.
The talk of the west and it's no jest, for they crowded near to see,
The man who trimmed the horsemen's hair, while his stock was running free.

The races began on a Monday, so he wandered on down to the gap
And fetched that Chatahoochee mare for the 'naugural Handicap.
He was oh so smug for he also drug that raw-boned colt called Jake
For he'd perform that afternoon in the meeting's only stake.

He tethered 'em both to a big oak tree and pulled burrs from their tails
And told the jock when he threw him up "No sense to use a nail,
Just plain horse sense, stay near the fence, and ride like Wild Bill Cody
And steer this colt around the turns or he'll run to Pokolodie."

There's no need to relate the wonderful fate befell that afternoon
When Chatahoochee set his sights for fortune on the moon.
That rugged pair did win for fair, and to the tune of a carefree song,
The barber sat in his chair and grinned "How long has this been goin' on?"

The winner's take gave him a stake so he vowed that very night
To campaign stock as black as death and too with stockings white.
He travelled wide for the stock he vied and they ran to expectation,
For many a year were without peer throughout our Western nation.

But times did come when they ran like bums and drained that barber's poke,
Of stock bereft, just one horse left, he realized he was broke.
Yet he hustled a job on a horse car, and stowed his horse on after dark,
'Twas thus he managed passage to the meet at Dufferin Park.

Illustration by Dianne Horton Barnsley

Old Carhan King, the last of the string, got Chatahoochee out of hock,
For he broke the record to Dufferin Park from the C.N. railway dock.
And the books will show that he got the dough on three successive tries
At the bull ring track where he started back and really showed those guys.

The trainman believed he'd been deceived as he stood on the loading dock,
For he spotted a good-looking runner, with the rest of the heavy stock.
"I've tallied them twice and counted right, how come there's twenty-three?
Methinks that black with the blazed face came east on the rails for free."

Old Carhan King, the last of the string, got Chatahoochee out of hock,
For he broke the record to Dufferin Park from the C.N. railway dock.
And the books will show that he got the dough on three successive tries
At the bull ring track where he started back and really showed those guys.

And still out on the flatlands where oil wells gush so free,
They talk of Chatahoochee's mare and the days that used to be;
And where the golden wheatlands wave like seas of prairie grass,
They spin this tale o'er pints of ale, the good days of the past.

This is the tale that was told to me by a gyp with snow-white hair,
In a shakedown bed, right under the shed of Big Jim Fair.
The waves of Lake Ontario could be heard as they lashed the shore,
As he spun this yarn, 'neath the old frame barn, inside the feedroom door.

THE BALLAD OF BILL THE REVEREND

The Ballad of Bill the Reverend

There's a story that needs telling,
It concerns the racetrack breed,
'Bout a gyp named Bill the Reverend
And St. Gregory his steed.

'Twas winter at the Dufferin
And things were mighty tough,
For 'Reverend' and a big bay horse
He'd purchased on the cuff.

Bill scurried in the mornings
To make a buck or two,
By mucking stalls and walking hots,
Like all the hustlers do,

But jobs were few and dollars too,
And so, alas it fell
The 'Reverend' thought of stealing oats
For his equine pal.

And all the time St. Gregory
Just stood there munching hay,
While Willie figured ways and means
Of keeping things that way.

The Ballad of Bill the Reverend

The old bay horse just stood there
Contented in his stall,
While the 'Reverend' was conniving -
His back up to the wall.

A coffee for his breakfast,
Bran mash at dinner time,
Stewed carrots for his supper,
With a little dago wine.

Tho' the essence of his vittles
Induced to malnutrition,
'Twas not the cause of poor ole Bill's
Being close to all perdition.

As he lay with empty belly
In his shakedown bed a-scheming,
He dozed off for a minute
And promptly went to dreaming;
Of boyhood days when he had the craze -
A horse to call his own,
A racetrack life (no loving wife) —
A tackroom for a home.

But his Daddy was a parson
Who daily racked his brain
With logic and with reason
In an effort to explain,
"You're an only son of mine my lad
And it's you obligation
To study for the ministry -
A hallowed occupation.

The Ballad of Bill the Reverend

Besides you are a young 'un
And it's up to me, your father,
To see that you don't do the things,
You really hadn't orter.
The ministry's your calling,
I wish you wouldn't balk,
When I am old and useless
You'll be caring for the flock.

And when you fill your daddy's shoes
Be sure to recollect,
'Tis your moral obligation
All peoples to protect;
The poor and needy are the ones,
Who need a helping hand,
Whatever faith they practice -
From any foreign land."

At this point Bill awakened,
But lay there for a while,
'Tho his stomach gnawed from hunger,
The 'Reverend' had a smile.
'Tho things looked mighty gloomy –
Could almost say 'done in'
The 'Reverend's' smile just widened -
Into a happy grin.

Then straightaway he fetched a pail
And water from the spicket,
And hummed a tune (Gregorian Chant),
As clear as any cricket.
"Dear father thank you for the thought,
I'm on my way to see
If all the parsons are as kind
As you'd want me to be."

He walked awhile and looked around
Until a parsonage he found,
Quickly introduced himself
To parson, who devoid of wealth,
Listened to his tale of woe,
Attentively and with show
Of understanding for the need
Of Willie and his hungry steed.

Immediately he saw the light
Of Bill the Reverend's sorry plight,
Acknowledging his near demise
Offered him a compromise;
Half-interest in the Thoroughbred
Who'd put poor Willie in the red,
For Bill had almost guaranteed
Potential of his running steed.

The Ballad of Bill the Reverend

The parson looked a trifle pale
When he'd signed the Bill of Sale.
Now in legal partnership
With Bill the Reverend - a racetrack gyp;
He wondered if the congregation
Would approve incorporation,
'Cause vittles for the parson's table
Were cheaper than a public stable.

Yet springtime came to the Dufferin course
And Gregory was a runnin' horse,
Carrying the silks of the Rectory
To many a smashing victory.
The investment reaping large returns,
'Cause Gregory skipped 'round the turns,
And thus he kindly reimbursed
The congregation's empty purse.

The days that followed proved to be
Successful for the 'company';
Bill the Reverend's jubilation
Matched that of the congregation,
For when St. Gregory ran his races
The congregation's happy faces
Wagered heavily, (as a rule),
Increasing Orpen's mutuel pool.

The days that followed proved to be

Successful for the 'company'.

Bill the Reverend's jubilation

Matched that of the congregation,

For when St. Gregory ran his races

The congregation's happy faces

Wagered heavily, (as a rule),

Increasing Orpen's mutuel pool.

The Ballad of Bill the Reverend

Yet Gregory did pull up sore
And to the 'Reverend' - nevermore,
The congregation's noble steed,
(Which Willie once had guaranteed)
Would carry silks of the Rectory,
To a running race - and victory.
For the Vet explained as he made his test,
"He's a 'broke-down' horse who's done his best."

Today there stands in a Bloor Street church,
Where you and all may see,
A statue of a Saint whose name
Is good St. Gregory.
And when the people pass it by,
(so reverently of course)
I know they think of Dufferin Park -
And Bill the Reverend's horse.

The Ballad of Hank the Gyp

This is the song of Hank the Gyp as he rests in his shakedown bed,
In straw and hay, death-like he lay, a gunny sack pillowed his head.
'Twas a fearful plight on a winter's night, and this is what he said.

"I'm one of the horsemen's brotherhood,
And have been all my life,
I've sweated and toiled with the worst of stock
And never had a wife.
I've followed my dreams and tho' it seems,
Have had my share of loot,
'Twas the hard-earned bucks those dogies earned,
And I never cared a hoot.

Look at my crippled body,
Each bone in my frame's been broke.
Look at the mare in the stall next door,
And look in my empty poke.
Look at this barren feedroom,
Look at the tack so worn,
Yet 'ere I ship to the Big Shedrow,
Another horseman's born.

This racing is only a gamble,
The worst is as good as the best.
I rode with the tops of an era,
And should have come out like the rest.
With Loftus, McIver and Sande,
Oh God but it's awful to think,
The thousands of dollars I've squandered,
On gambling, women and drink.

Those days of the past weren't meant to last,
When we rode for ten per cent,
We parlayed hundreds to thousands,
And led the life of a gent.
Yet ask any man who remembers
And he'll bet you the best in his string,
That our sin was the strength of desire,
And we only desired to win.

We were just like one big family
And lived as a breed apart,
A wild and reckless, carefree life,
(That's how I got my start).
Money was just like dirt then,
Easy to get and to spend,
But we had the bug and a whiskey jug
Got us in the end.

Forty years on the racetrack,
Trying my best to keep
The rep that I made as a punker,
But ever I sink so deep.
Gyping about on the bull rings
In search of a pot of gold;
Forty years on the racetrack,
Forty years, and I'm old.

The Ballad of Hank the Gyp

Old and weak but no matter,
There's a spider left in the jug.
I'll hustle the jock's mount tomorrow
And ride a kid with the bug.
The ole mare'll win tomorrow,
Win by a country mile,
We'll bet a hundred across the board
To keep us for a while.

"Come Jock, the Judge said 'riders up'."
Climb aboard and tie your knot,
Tuck her in 'til the quarter pole,
This big one means a lot.

Reach and clout her at the eighth pole,
Then fold up and hand ride a bit
And she'll whip these bums in the Handicap,
Or my name's not Hank the Gyp."

This was the song of Hank the Gyp as he lay in a shakedown bed.
In straw and hay, death-like he lay, a gunny sack pillowed his head.
The old mare nickered for breakfast oats, but Hank the Gyp was dead.

The Giant Killer

Little bay horse with rugged coat
And heart of solid gold,
'Ere the butcher points a bullet,
Your story will be told.

Your Ma was a 'broke-down' plater,
Your Pop of outlaw breed;
You look like an Indian pony,
Your heart is the source of your speed.

To run was your only desire
With pedigreed equines of worth.
You ran and you won your breeding
Each time they tightened the girth.

And when Mr. Handicapper
Packed lead on your ill-shaped back,
You heeded the challenge with courage,
You won and carried the pack.

Today you are only a plater,
Long years have levelled your speed,
You've broken a bone in your stifle,
No longer can earn your feed.

They've ordered a van for you only,
And soon you'll traverse the trail,
Where broken down Thoroughbreds travel
When old and useless and frail.

You've enriched your enervate owners,
Insurance will glut their greed;
You're a cripple and only a burden,
Good only for canine feed.

The Giant Killer

Yet in the hearts that remember the gallant
Your feats will remain in place,
And, perhaps, out-live your owners,
Who have sent you to shame and disgrace.

A Thoroughbred by your record
Your masters have trophies you've won.
If only their hearts could acquire
The spirit that made you run.

Only a Dud

Of fashionable breed your mother,
Your pop a reputable stud;
You've tried to live up to your breeding,
But, alas, you're only a dud.

You are staked in the finest of races,
Your coat shines with dapples galore,
Knee-deep in good straw you are bedded;
Your name is inscribed on your door.

Your owners are wealthy and loving,
They deem you the best of a breed;
And as long as their bankroll is handy,
You'll never be wanting for feed.

On stakes day you're led to the Paddock,
Where punters peer over the fence.
They whisper one another,
"What beauty and elegance."

Yet afraid to wager a dollar
For of talents they're fully aware;
Equine beauty's a stirring sight,
But 'to cash' is the reason they're there.

You'll live a long life and be happy
In paddocks Utopian,
But you're not worth a counterfeit nickel,
You'll never be worth a damn.

George the Goose

'Way back before the days when night watchmen were hired to patrol Woodbine's shedrows, there was a two-legged feathered fellow who watched over trainer Dick Townrow's shedrow both day and night. A goose, affectionately known as George, was the stable's mascot, and he vehemently protected his turf against all intruders. And, many unsuspecting visitors to Townrow's stable incurred George's wrath.

Shortly after Dick Townrow passed away in the early 1960s, George was found dead in the very shedrow he had protected for so many years. No one knows whether he died of grief at the loss of his master, or whether he met his fate at the hands of someone who had incurred his wrath.

Come gather 'round boys and don't vamoose
'Til I tell the story of George the Goose.
He walks the shed both day and night
Which we all agree is that goose's right.

Now there's a young man who we all know
Whom that rascal goose dealt an awful blow,
'Cause he teased that gander and made him sizzle,
'Til he made for him like a guided missile.

The scar still remains on that young man's bean,
A souvenir of the battle scene.
The moral of this story you all know,
Beware of the goose of Dick Townrow.

Shortly after this poem was published, George was found dead one morning in Dick Townrow's shedrow.

George the Goose
A Eulogy

Although there have been many
Who have departed from our midst,
We all admit that George the Goose
Will be most sorely missed.

It's funny just how one as he
Can creep into our hearts,
And maybe shed a tear or two
As George the Goose departs.

He is gone but not forgotten
By the men along the shed,
Who've watched him strut along the shed
And cock his goose's head.

And if God, in his wisdom,
Has made a gooses' heaven,
We're sure that George will be there
And wake each morn at seven.

And when he roams about, above,
In those celestial places,
He'll think about, and yearn, I'm sure,
To be back at the races.

George the Goose

He'll see the horses going
From the stables to the track,
And many of his shedrow pals
With mucksacks on their back.

He'll hear the bugle blowing
And the sounds of horses' feet,
And the thunderous roar of racing fans
When they cheer and stamp their feet.

He'll recall strutting along the shedrow
With slow and measured pace,
With watchful eyes that captured all
That's happening in that place.

He'll see the quiet gelding
Who was once an ornery stud,
And the dappled, lop-eared filly
Who broke her maiden in the mud.

He'll hear the little chestnut mare
As she squeals in joyful glee,
When handsome colts prance by her stall
They roar back in ecstasy.

He'll see Butch, the jockey agent,
Who brought him tidbits every day,
And the Vet who cared for his equine pals
And the feedman who brought hay.

He'll see the big black stallion,
Who wouldn't pass a filly in a race,
And Skyline Scotty heading for
Libations at that place.

Now Townrow's boys were George's pals
And they vowed it only fitting,
That George be buried, proper like,
In a manner that was fitting.

They wrapped George in a gunny sack.
And close to Woodbine's inside rail,
They buried George in a shallow grave
And hereby lies this tale.

'Tis said that George is sometimes seen
In the misty light of dawn,
As jocks breeze down the backstretch,
With their trainers looking on.

Yes, sometimes in the morning's light
When the jocks go galloping by
They've spotted George as he struts about
With his head up to the sky.

El Perfecto

Avelino Gomez – the very name excited Canadian racing fans. The fiery Cuban known to horsemen as 'El Perfecto', dominated the Canadian racing scene for more than 20 years, He was born in Cuba in 1928, won 4,055 races and was North America's leading race-winning jockey in 1966. In Canada, Gomez was untouchable. In 1966, he became the first jockey in Canadian racing to win 300 races in a single season. He was six times Canada's top rider and won the Queen's Plate a record four times. Racing fans remember him for his patented victorious high leaps from the saddle in the winner's circle. He was inducted into the Canadian Horse Racing Hall of Fame in 1977.

Avelino Gomez died from injuries suffered in a spill at Woodbine in the 25th running of Canadian Oaks in 1980.

Just a Cuban Caballero who performs each day with zest,
Humping horses to the wire in the way that he knows best.
He rides to win amidst the din, although we boo and shout,
A fine and polished rider, of that there is no doubt.

When he comes from out the hunt and boots one home in front,
He's our hero and cause of our elation.
When we've cashed a winning ticket at the fifty dollar wicket,
We cheer him with a wonderful ovation.

But even when he's beaten there is no such thing as cheatin',
It's a tough and grueling contest to the wire.
He'll tan 'em to the hair and do everything that's fair,
Just to satisfy our innermost desire.

His percentage is the highest, so let us not be biased
When we blow a bet and hang our heads in sorrow;
For he'll ride another winner when our bankroll is much thinner.
Remember, there is always a tomorrow.

The Call of the Shedrow

Have you gazed along the shedrow at the horsemen and the horses?
Have you wandered to the railing at the nation's leading courses?
Have you often had the feeling that you own a horse, and still,
There is something sorely missing - a gap you just can't fill?

Have you ever watched a guinea with mucksack on his back?
Have you sometimes looked with envy at the riders on the track?
Have you often wished the hotwalker were you instead of he?
Do you long to bunk in a tackroom bed as a gypsy and be free?

Have you oft espied a guinea and thought how sore you lack?
And gazed with admiration as he snuggly fit the tack?
On occasion have you wondered how he keeps those dapples shining?
And long to do the things he does…is this what you are pining?

Although you are a man of wealth, would you really like to know
How the man who tends your equine friend is going to treat his bow?
And what will he prescribe and treat for your charge's tummy ache,
And what endearing words for him when he runs and wins the stake?

The Call of the Shedrow

Illustration by Elaine Macpherson

Do you look at your colourbearer as he stands there in his stall,
And feel that you're inadequate, 'cause you don't know him at all?
Do you long to work upon his coat with rubrag and with brush?
And pack his feet with care each day to ease the pain of thrush?

Are you wont to leave your shiny desk, as they say, 'just pack it in',
And learn to ply a blister to the colt who bucked his shins?
Do you really yearn to 'get under one', arise to turfdoms heights,
Rub on tendons 'til your arms ache, and snug those lily whites?

Illustration by Elaine Macpherson

Do you relish the thought of pulling manes, or braiding tails for mud?
To apply a ring or cage, what e'er, for some big ornery stud?
Would you like to pull the caps off for the baby in the barn?
Do you long to break the yearlings that you have up on the farm?

The Call of the Shedrow

Would you rather be a hotwalker and journey to the left?
Bet your case deuce on the big hoss, with no eatin' money left?
Would you not trade your millions, just for a little while,
To walk, or rub or train one…or gallop one a mile?

Would you gyp about the bull rings and hustle for the feed?
Would you ship to the Big Apple 'cause you think your horse has speed?
Would you gamble on a gamble, a plug with four bad wheels?
Be banned for over-zealousness - then return and make appeals?

Would you take a cripple on the cuff and nurse him to a race?
Go without your evenin' meal when you bet and blow the race?
Would you hustle for the jock's mount and whether win or lose,
Have a little extra for a jug, some cheap but potent booze?

Would you like to be a racetracker, just for a year or two,
To struggle, and to lead the life that many horsemen do?
To sleep in shakedown beds at times, whenever the going's rough,
Yet take the chance to live it up, when things just aren't so tough?

It's only a thought I offer you, yet would most not beguile
To leave their fancy offices and join us for a while.
To struggle and to triumph, and always grasp at glory,
Re-write a chapter of their lives…into a horseman's story.

Empty Tack

Sturdy tack, now on the shelf,
Image of my former self,
Symbol of my lustrous past,
Tool of trade success you cast.

Once you had a valet's care,
Money, yes, we had our share.
We basked in limelight, high esteem
Was ours, yes, we were a team.

Riding eight a day with zest,
Opined by experts to be best.
Shaking hands of the Royal clan,
Honour achieved by a little man.

Tonight again, perhaps we'll ride
In retrospect, mounts bonafide;
Tho' owners proud, incensed with glee,
Will never pay the riding fee.

Illustration by John Verdura

The Revenge of Puss n Boots

A humourous look at the real-life story of Canada's famous swimming horse.

"All his past fame was forgotten,
he was called a bloomin' fake,
'Ere since he dumped his rider
and went swimming in the lake."

Puss n Boots

On Saturday, September 2, 1961, before a crowd of 14,106 racing fans at Fort Erie Race Track, a strapping bay colt named Puss n Boots wrote his name into Canadian racing lore when he dumped his rider and plunged into one of the track's infield lakes.

Puss n Boots was leading by five lengths at the head of the stretch in the seven-furlong turf event when he darted through an opening in the hedge along the rail and slid into the lake, much to the chagrin and bewilderment of jockey Ronnie Behrens.

Five days before the colt had sped to his maiden victory in his first lifetime start with an easy 11-length tally over Fort Erie's dirt course with Ronnie Behrens aboard.

The boys who worked on the starting gate rushed across the infield to the rescue, as did Coldwater Bob, the colt's groom. Bob jumped into a small boat docked on shore and some of the starting gate crew pushed him out into the lake, but they failed to give him the oars, which were lying on the shore.

The starting gate boys stripped down and swam towards Puss n Boots, but each time someone got near, he shied away from them. And, he was getting tired. Trainer Frank Merrill, who had arrived on the scene, was worried that his charge would drown, but eventually the big colt was coaxed to safety.

Fort Erie Race Track, sometimes referred to as the most picture-perfect racetrack in the world with its scenic infield flowers and lakes, became even more famous on that day, and Puss n Boots became its greatest celebrity. He made *Ripley's Believe It or Not, Esquire Magazine*, and almost every newspaper and horse racing magazine in America.

The entire episode was captured on film by Bobby Bruce, who was operating the track's film patrol camera that day.

Puss n Boots was foaled on April 7, 1959 at Pin Oaks Farm in Versailles, Kentucky. He was purchased as part of three-horse package for $22,000 by Roxie Gian of Buffalo, N.Y.

Frank Merrill Jr., the colt's trainer, said he had trained more than 4,000 horses, but admitted he was best known as the trainer of Puss n Boots.

"He was my 'Wonder Horse", Merrill told Louis Cauz, in an interview, "because for a while there, I wondered what he was going to do next.

"He was a victim of circumstance. Always something would happen, but it was never really his fault. He had freak accidents. His life was full of freak accidents."

From the day he bought him out of a farmer's field, Puss n Boots demonstrated an uncanny familiarity with disaster. And, thirty years later, Merrill's life rarely passed without a reference to Puss n Boots.

Puss n Boots went on to win the Display Stakes at Greenwood that year, and at three raced against some of the continent's finest sophomores during a 25-race campaign.

At four, the long legged colt with the white star was a model of correct deportment, finishing first or second 13 times in 22 races. He defeated good horses in the Autumn Stakes and posted an upset victory over some of America's finest turf campaigners with Ron Turcotte in the saddle in the Niagara Stakes at Fort Erie, the meet's closing day feature in 1963. The victory was a sweet payback for disappointing Fort Erie fans with his plunge into the infield lake as a two-year-old.

At five, Puss n Boots developed aches and pains, but still equalled the course record while winning Fort Erie's Fair Play Stakes, boosting his lifetime bank account to just under $90,000. But his days of running against top allowance horses were over.

At seven, Puss n Boots ran in claiming races, but the same season was retired to Merrill's farm where he was trained to be a jumper. That too, was a disastrous experiment. Merrill then brought him back to the races, but he was claimed, and it was mostly downhill from then on.

Puss n Boots made his final career start on August 20, 1969 before a crowd of 5,000 at the fairgrounds in South Weymouth, Massachusetts. He broke from the outside post and was just a couple of lengths off the pace at the top of the stretch when suddenly his right foreleg snapped. It was an ignominious conclusion of a capricious career. Removed from his glamorous past, his demise was that of a long-forgotten celebrity. His epilogue, written by the chart caller for the Daily Racing Form, said: "Puss n Boots enjoyed prominence until just inside the stretch when he broke down in the right fore."

Today, the life and legend of Puss n Boots lives on at Fort Erie Race Track in Fort Erie, Ontario. The Puss n Boots Cup is raced in his memory each year. And, each year, in a reversal of roles, the winning jockey (and sometimes the winning trainer) of the event, takes a swim in the same lake that Puss n Boots paddled about in, in 1961.

Taken from a story by Louis Cauz on the colourful career and life of Frank H. Merrill (1919 - 1990).

The Revenge of Puss n Boots

There were saddened hearts at Erie for a month or even more,
There were stifled oaths and curses - every racing fan was sore.
Can't figure why a classy nag should be so assinine,
With all us fine folk putting so much money on the line.

All his past fame was forgotten, he was called a bloomin' fake,
Ere since he dumped his rider and went swimming in the lake.
They called him 'Aqua Charlie' and you must admit it suits,
That running, jumping, swimming steed they once called Puss n Boots.

But fate is kind and oftentimes it even smiles on horses,
A second chance for equine blood on Erie's racing courses.
On closing day his big chance lay, to deal that lethal blow,
For 'Aqua Charlie' to regain his former status quo.

All Erie had assembled, ten thousand fans with dough,
From Welland County, Hamilton and throngs from Buffalo,
To view the annual running of Fort Erie's Niagara Stakes,
One mile and three around the turf, close to the infield lakes.

The bugler's trumpet summoned forth the valued equine beauty,
Who would strain each limb and sinew for the laurels and the booty.
But in that mob of thousands there was not a single yell
To root for 'Aqua Charlie' – no one to wish him well.

Instead they booed and jibed him for the memory was plain,
But he threw his head and kicked his heels and snorted in disdain.
His eyes were bright and fiery – and he pricked his ears with glee
As he broke 'way from his pony for one and all to see.

At this time it should be mentioned that some equines of repute
Had shipped from Saratoga for the trophy and the loot;
For pots of such enormity will buy a lot of hay,
So thought the owners of Pollingfold, and also Marlin Bay.

When the Starter sprung the latch, Puss n Boots was on his way,
He fought his way through the gruelling pack – it truly was his day.
In a sweep of muscle, strained and taught, he ran with gallant stride,
Today no jock was needed on this history-making ride.

The Revenge of Puss n Boots

At the head of the lane he made his run, right to the leader's girth,
And then went on in a jump or two, to gain the winner's berth.
And at the point where in days gone by — he made that grave mistake,
He did not glance to either side - not even at the lake.

Today there'll be no swimming, for I must regain my name,
I'll dispel my lowbrow moniker and shed that awful shame.
I'll bask in flashbulb limelight and once again restore
The favour of the thousand fans - that once I had before.

Ten thousand eyes were on him as he entered victory lane,
Five thousand tongues applauded, as he tossed his silky mane.
Tho' few of them had backed him, they rejoiced with gleeful cries,
'Cause Puss n Boots regained his name, the victory and the prize.

Oh, somewhere in this grandstand place some throw away their tickets,
And somewhere here some stand to cash at fifty dollar wickets,
But everywhere fans speak with pride, in manner so sedate;
Fort Erie hearts are happy now - their horse has won the stake.

What Might Have Been

The racing season is my friends
In the late and final stages
When we must ask what has been done
With all our summer's wages.

And many other things, no doubt,
Turn over in our mind,
And try in vain to answer all
The queries of this kind.

What happened to the two-year-old
Who showed such promise in the spring?
To the only Plate horse in the barn
Who never made it to the ring?

Why were we beaten noses
And could never win a pot?
And owners always sing the blues
With all the dough they've got.

What happened to the yearling
For whom the boss gave all his loot?
He wound up on the Vet's List,
And popped a splint to boot.

How come we hit a muddy track
When it looked like the mare could win?
It could have been my best year yet.
When I think what might have been.

Out on the plain midst wind and rain I herded with the best,
And oft at night, with wolves in sight (believe me it's no jest);
I hummed a tune to my friend the moon, as those wooly critters bleated,
And prayed to God on Western sod, for the times that I had cheated.

Illustration by Dianne Horton Barnsley

The Ballad of Sheepherder Bill

The wind blew through the crevices of our tackroom walls that night.
We were bedded down in a vacant stall and the moon shone big and bright.
The backstretch of ole Stamford Park was quiet as a jail,
'Cept for the occasional rattle of an empty water pail.

The mare had run her race that day, we'd bet our loot and won,
And just returned from Niagara Falls where we had a little fun.
Our bottle was almost empty, a spider did remain,
Which we'd consume next morning to relieve a gnawing pain.

We lay there just a talking, 'cause none of us could sleep;
Especially Sheepherder Bill who tried at counting sheep.
I lay there just a thinking, when suddenly arose,
A most important question which at Willie I did pose.

A pal of mine for many years and oft I query still,
How come he got the moniker of 'Ole Sheepherder Bill'?
A man who'd rubbed the finest, and worked for Nipper Rowe,
Should have a name more fittin', you must admit it's so.

I raised my head right out of bed of barley-perfumed straw,
And set my bony hands around my squarely pointed jaw.
Sez I to Bill "Why is it, you are tagged with such a name?
Tell the story of your christening and relate who is to blame".

The Ballad of Sheepherder Bill

'Twas then and there with vivid stare, I lay too all aghast,
As Willie told the story of his wild and wooly past.
His tale was all so life-like that I oft recall it yet.
'Ere since the night he told me, the night we won the bet.

Sez Bill, "The whole thing started, oh so many years ago,
I had a mare named Mighty Fine and trained her in the snow.
Those years were good, we all had food, yet good things cannot last",
'Twas thus that Willie delved into his history of the past.

"In those days I had money, believe me it's no lie,
And dearly loved to dine upon a dish called shepherd's pie.
A glutton for mutton was I then, and Belanger made it best;
Partook of it morn and evening, every plate with zest.

"Then sudden as fate would have it, (the old mare had given her best);
We packed up our traps and belongings and quietly shipped out West.
'Twas a blessing by far, she died in the boxcar, that plucky mare of mine;
So I peddled the tack and made my track to the next farm up the line.

"'Tho I hated cows I made my vows that ne'er more I'd return,
To a racetrack life of toil and strife and a lesson I did learn.
So I took the cure ('twas the farmer's lure), to a life of herding sheep,
And played the part, 'tho at the start, it hurt me 'way down deep.

"Out on the plain midst wind and rain I herded with the best,
And oft at night, with wolves in sight (believe me it's no jest);
I hummed a tune to my friend the moon, as those wooly critters bleated,
And prayed to God on Western sod, for the times that I had cheated.

"I felt as Cain and wished in vain that I hadn't been so hasty,
For oft I thought of the times I'd bought that shepherd's pie, so tasty.
Here I am with the big-horned ram, a caring for the flock,
Them all ringed in a circle, me sittin' on a rock.

"But springtime comes when sheep and bums shed wool and jobs, alike.
Picked up a mare with winter hair and headed down the pike.
She was big and strong and 'twasn't long 'til she proved that she was fit.
The boys all joked "There's Sheepherder Bill", but it mattered not a bit.

"Since then, I've been back to my home on the track, and the place where I belong;
To my racetrack life of toil and strife, and tho' it might be wrong;
I'm here to stay for many a day – so do not query still,
That's how I got the moniker of 'Ole Sheepherder Bill'."

Illustration by Kit Mo

Memory Lane

Many a night by a tackroom light
We've sat and spun our tales,
And fell asleep, in slumber deep
On a bed of wired bales.

For Pete and I in days gone by
Travelled life's road together,
Were blessed with fame and then with shame,
Just two birds of a feather.

Yet we recall the cheers of all
As we humped one to the wire.
We rode to win and our only sin
Was the strength of our desire.

Those days are past, they couldn't last,
The loot went to our heads.
For booze and gals and freeloadin' pals
Have made our hustlers' beds.

There's nothing now and that I vow
But memories that we treasure,
Of gals and steeds and hustlers' needs,
And drink that's been our measure.

Memory Lane

Tho' friends are few and dollars, too,
We've stories by the dozens,
As we spin queer tales on musty bales
Of our own fraternal cousins.

There was Boxcar Bill McEwan
And Mucksack Jack, a gyp;
And, you'll recall old Gashouse Mike,
Ye gads, he was a pip.

Do you remember Nervy Nat
Or Pokolodie Red?
When Cowboy Parker met his fate,
Was robbed and left for dead?

Was on a binge with Lyin' Sam,
I do recall it well.
We wound up on the tow ring
At the old Cross Bar Hotel.

Silk Hat Harry was a card,
And so was Mickey Fallon,
And Sitting Bull who sat around,
Drank whiskey by the gallon.

I shan't forget Three-Finger-Dick,
Or even Teapot Tim,
Or cease to wonder at the gun
Of old Missouri Jim.

Mechanical Jack has left our midst,
And Tuppence and Looking Glass Frank
Have joined a pal in the great beyond,
In the person of Handlebar Hank.

Society Red has passed away
And so has Paddy the Priest;
Michigan Ike has shipped upstairs
And Goat Eye is deceased.

So many more I have in store,
But if with your permission.
Just wait again 'til I wet my pen,
It's just an intermission.

A Horseman's Prayer

Sitting alone in a canvas chair
Under the shed one night,
I heard a horseman say his prayers
In the dark of summer's night.

And as he rambled on, he said
"Oh Lord please hear my call
For I've travelled our fair circuit
From Windsor to Montreal.

"The meetings were much shorter then,
But they took their toll on me.
I'm ready to ship to my resting place
'Cause I've paid the entrance fee.

"Have been a gyp most all my life,
But Lord that's not a sin,
Just let me last 'til the meeting's out
'Cause the old mare's gonna win.

Been doing a lot of thinking Lord,
Of the meeting you run up there,
So please Mr. Handicapper
Won't you listen to my prayer?

"A horseman's heaven is to me
Where all us folk can happy be.
A place where men of every creed
Can run his horse and buy good feed.

"Where every racing strip is fast
And horses shoes don't wear, but last.
Where handicappers in their plight
Don't pack the weight – but make it light.

"Where every steed can run its race
And pay big odds for Win and Place.
Where riders have good hands and seat,
And Duffis' pickings hard to beat.

"Where every Steward's fair and just
And every shedrow free from dust;
Adorned with grass and trees and flowers
And friends to while away the hours.

A Horseman's Prayer

"Where every tackroom's clean and bright
All air-conditioned to sleep at night.
Where trainers all can happy be
Abiding rules of the O.R.C.

"Where hotwalkers, guineas and everyone
Can do their work and have some fun.
Please grant these things I do implore
As I have often asked before.

"In virtues Lord I am most poor,
But of one thing you can be sure,
I've fed my steeds the very best
And helped to fill a race, when asked.

"So please dear Lord consider this
My one-stall application.
Grant to this old and tired gyp
A meet of long duration."

I Go Me Once to Race Track Place

A new immigrant to Canada goes to the races for the first time.

I go me once to race track place
Dat one dey call Woodbine.
Me ride the bus from Bay and Queen
De weather it was fine.

An all de udder peeples
In dat beeg omnibus,
Wuz scrutinizing Wall Street -
A Raisen Form it was.

Me tinks, sez I, 'tis wunnerful
To be with dese fine folk
Who deal in high finances,
By gar she is no joke.

De man who sit beside me
Have very good connexions.
He tole me who de winners was,
Hees very own zelections.

Dis guy, hees name is Meester Tout,
He's leetle man and slim,
I know hees name is Tout because
Dey all call "tout" at heem.

I Go Me Once To Race Track Place

Dem peeples must be very rich
Why no dere money shows?
And some dey look like homberlie
And some wit funny clothes.

An den anudder man he say
"Ole Mamie beat me nose."
Dis guy should wed ole contry gal
An not take all dem blows.

Dat omnibus she finally stop
Bezide wan beeg high fence;
Some beeg ole gal try knock me down,
By gar I tak offence.

Dem leetle gals in uniform
Who geev us all some ticket,
Was wery nice so why folks scairt
And run to man at wicket.

For yus wen dey got tru de gate
Dey run like asternot.
Me come to see de horses run
Lees dat wat I thought.

An all dem guys in granstan place
Give tickets – real nice fellas,
Wit funny names lak Place and Show,
And wan dey call "Quinella".

But deres a guy I lak de bes
Doubles Daily eez heez name;
Pore man he yus get dat wan try
Me tink it eez a shame.

Dey let give tickets only once
No treat lak all de rest,
He work lak crazee at the first,
I know he do heez best.

Bezides, he geeve big chanz to win,
Two try instead of one,
Wit beeg return on money
Two 'orse for price of one.

De Meester Place and Show okay,
Quinella, too much trouble,
But I come back 'ere every week
To get me Daily Double.

Times to Remember

To this scribe, the racetrack is a fascinating place, full of great human interest stories and colourful shedrow characters. Turning back the pages of time, I fondly recall sitting over a cup of coffee in Leo Belanger's Greenwood track kitchen, back in the 1950s, with such fine gentlemen of the turf as Mose Dunn, Jim Smith, Chic Ross and Frank Higgins. Their conversation often turned to some of the many horsemen, who at one time were cogs in the big wheel of Thoroughbred racing. As they fanned the embers of the past, I managed to catch some of the names and places mentioned.

They discussed one Side Door Harry and Stick Pin Chappy too,
Commented on the recipe of Greasy Charlie's stew.
They recall ole Hairbreadth Harry, look back in retrospect,
The time when Jim Fair won the Plate, in tuxedo and top hat decked.

They conjure up their memories, retrace back through the years,
Reminiscing on an all-time great in the person of R.J. Speers.
They summon forth old relics and fresh their thoughts renew,
And bring to mind one Toothless Joe and Can't Win Smitty, too.

From out the past they recollect, and no one will refute
That Mobile Larry was a groom and hustler of repute.
Their talk is an education for they have at their fingers ends,
A wealth of racetrack history as the discourse slowly wends.

They rake the ashes of the past, recall in twenty-eight,
When Marshall Cassidy was the man and Starter at the Gate.
Their memories are awakened as they reminisce anew,
On Peg Leg Randall, Parlay Slim and Centrefield Willie, too.

The Tourist, king of the bootleggers, Mousy Watts and Mechanical Jack,
Topics of fond old memories, as the pages of time roll back.
They talked of Tea Bag McCullough, recalled one Whitey the Pest,
And all agreed in solemn tones that Jim's I.C.R.A was best.

There's nought like a bit of caffeine (but not in its purest state)
To stimulate an old timers brain, like a racetrack kitchen debate.
For the young all sit with open mouths, and their noggins insatiate,
As the sages of our city speak, yes those of the hairless pate.

Tho' bereft of original choppers, and hair that's turned to gray,
They've made their mark and earned it, and it wasn't earned in a day.
And, 'though the sagas of backstretch lore through the years have gone unwritten,
It behooves to pen a line or two, in a manner that's befittin'.

Illustration by Elaine Macpherson

This Jock's First Ride

This rousing tale which I confide
Is 'bout a jock and his first ride;
My very first mount, my very first horse,
'Round Woodbine's grassy Marshall Course.

Over the green all lined with hedge
And not far from the water's edge,
Where many a bug-boy's met disaster,
'Cause horses think the green's a pasture.
And those who do not care to eat
The vegetation at their feet,
Have oft decided as a whim
To venture forth and have a swim
Into Woodbine's flowered lakes,
Causing backers all to quake
And rather venture home to wife
Have followed suit to take their life.

It also must be quite a strain
On those poor chaps who try to train
For pompous owners in their boxes,
Think "'Tis a hunt, they're after foxes."

But wouldn't a jock feel mighty bitter
If he should find some ornery critter,
Which he has been engaged to ride
Should clear the hedge, and then decide
To romp about on Woodbine's grass
While all those bettors took the gas.

This Jock's First Ride

These were the thoughts passed through my noggin,
As postward with the pony joggin'
And with such thoughts as these in mind,
Was heartened that my horse went kind.
He pulled on the bit and pricked his ears,
He didn't sulk and showed no fears.
He was the veteran and I the pupil
Riding with jocks devoid of scruples.

We reached the gate, 'way down the chute
I thought 'Here's where I earn my loot.'
Took my place with pounding heart
And waited for the time to start;
Fear and excitement running high,
Chattering teeth and mouth bone dry,
To be left at the post on my first mount
Would just about be tantamount
To the end of a young and dear profession.
Must keep my head – no indiscretion.

The dark-haired Starter with thinnish face,
Hollered to groundmen "Take your place,
Come Angus seems you'll be of service
The jock on six looks mighty nervous.
Tong the three horse on the lip,
We've three to load and he's gonna flip."
Then looked at me "Hey you on eight,
We're loaded and now you make us wait,"
For my mount was frisky and turned his head,
My glee to be there had changed to dread.

This Jock's First Ride

The stud on the left began to paw,
The mare on the right had an iron jaw
And tried her best to snatch the rider
Out of the irons and down beside her.

The flag showed red and I cocked my whip,
Took a handful of mane and bit my lip.
With bells—a-ringing the gates sprung wide
And the soft green grass of the course outside,
Muffled the hoof beats of steeds that were bred
To run with the courage of sires, long dead.

One moment before my troubled mind
Was fearful to be left behind;
But now that the contest had begun,
Sensed that my mount was full of run.
Filling my eager heart with pride
He settled into a loping stride,
He pricked his ears and seemed to sense
My greenness, yet my confidence.

Bent on reaching the early lead
Went a big bay horse with a burst of speed,
Pulling his rider half over his head,
He jacked to the lead like a bull seeing red.
The rest of the field followed on in his wake,
Round that ribbon of green — not far from the lake.

Then the big chestnut stud with the figure-eight,
Who had caused such a ruckus at the gate
Tried to get through along the rail,
And he had his jock straight, but to no avail.

Illustration by Dianne Horton Barnsley

Down past the bleachers — just off to the right,
Stable hands hollered with all of their might,
Urging their charges and cussing the jock
And pointing out others who weren't too much stock.

Down past the bleachers – just off to the right,
Stable hands hollered with all of their might,
Urging their charges and cussing the jock
And pointing out others who weren't too much stock.
They'd honed on these beasts through Fort Erie mud,
And each was opining the other a dud.
One shouted "Hey jock, just stay out of trouble
You carry my wages, which I hope to double,
Watch for the dirt course, when you cross over,
From the grass to the dirt and on to the clover;
Where young horses swerve and old horses balk,
And many a favourite's stopped to a walk,
Or crashed through the hedge, or gone for a swim,
Just 'cause the jock was loose - lining him;
Or dropped his head when he went to the stick,
'Tis the very time they'll play you a trick."

The shouts from the bleachers died away
As I trailed the field down the straightaway;
Hoping that fate, to me would be kind
Trailing the field, three lengths behind,
Made me aware of the torrid pace
Leaving me and my mount in the post of disgrace.

Yet they had to slow down 'cause they'd sped such a burst
That some would be tiring and have to be nursed;
Yet to wait for the truth was trying for me,
The result of a contest which none can foresee.

Into the turn I felt my mount surging,
Picking up horses without any urging,
Pricking his ears and quickening stride,
He kept to the hedge and didn't go wide.

This Jock's First Ride

With the luck of a veteran I surely was gifted,
For I found myself seventh as three horses drifted;
Two others beside me were shortening stride,
And I knew 'twas the moment – the moment to ride.

The jock beside me seemed in a plight,
His mount saw the dirt course and flinched at the sight.
I hoped and I hoped that the beast would keep wide,
And thought what would come if he ducked in, or shied;
'Tho my mount paid no heed, my heart gave a thump,
For that critter 'longside me decided to jump
Over the dirt, in one long stride,
Which he didn't accomplish, I must confide.
Then he ducked in behind, 'tho his rider did swear.
Then he cleared the hedge nimbly and ran like a hare.

Down towards the lake their image grew dimmer,
'Tho bred for a runner, he looked like a swimmer,
For he jumped into the lake and he paddled about
While the jock who accompanied floundered about,
And I'm sure that his rider who swam in the drink
Thought as a Captain who'd had his boat sink.

From the grass to the dirt and again to the green,
The wire ahead, five horses between;
Where proud owners waited with praise for their steeds
And two-dollar bettors shouted their needs;
Where valets and guineas and trainers alike.
Shouted "Go" to their riders with all of their might;
To jocks who were scrubbing and honing their best,
Riding for victory, but meeting distress.

This Jock's First Ride

Then I swung my mount wide to the outside and clear
Where dead horses in front would not interfere,
For the last words I heard swinging into the tack,
Old Tex reeled off gruffly "There's plenty of track,
When you straighten for home at the head of the lane,
You'll have plenty of track, and a horse who is game.

"Just do as I taught you and finish strong,
And, oh, by the way, you're a hundred on.
With a ten-pound bug boy in the tack
We oughta be getting a few bucks back."

Clear of all trouble, my mount in full stride,
At last I'm a jockey, (a leg on each side);
Jacking on to the lead with a handful of horse,
Making history today on the Marshall Course.

Approaching the wire I posed for the people,
Cocked my toe like a veteran, felt tall as a steeple.
Then chalk-players rushed to the fence as I neared,
Booing the favourite, who'd plum disappeared,
Over the hedge and down towards the water,
And, at six-to-five he hadn't orter
Play tricks on folks who'd invested their savings,
'Twas awful, I tell you, the rants and the ravings.

While unhappy patrons showed their displeasure,
That horse in the lake swam around at his leisure.
Hoarse shouts echoed loud, and the rafters did quake,
I fear that tonight there'll be hats in the lake.

*Woodbine's Marshall Course was renamed the E.P. Taylor Turf Course in 1994.

The One Hundredth Running of the Queen's Plate

Photo by Michael Burns

On a mild grey day on June 30, 1959, Queen Elizabeth came to Woodbine for the one hundredth running of a race to which her great-great-grandmother had given royal assent a century before. E.P. Taylor's New Providence captured the run for the guineas that day. Above (l to r) Prince Philip, trainer Pete McCann, jockey Bobby Ussery, Queen Elizabeth, Mrs. Taylor and E.P. Taylor.

One century old, we've all been told, the Plate is here to stay,
Tradition, pomp and pageantry is why we're here today.
And those who've sallied forth to the Giant of the North,
Will witness all its fabulous array.

This race and all its glory is a chapter in the story,
For the men who've laid the structure of its worth.
Those who've kept it in existence, by their work and their persistence,
And endowed by royal patronage since birth.

A day of days, in many ways, the heirs of all its glory;
We stand before the finish line and wait,
For the one who'll set the pace and the victor of the race,
And the outcome which we all anticipate.

The One Hundredth Running of The Queen's Plate

When they're heading towards the post and we all begin to boast
Of the colt of our selection and desire;
And each heart begins to beat with the pounding of their feet,
As they round the turn and gallop to the wire.

When the laurels are presented, although we might resent it,
And throw away some tickets in despair.
A memory will remain that we always shall retain
Of this colourful and glorious affair.

And when the day is finished and the crowd has all diminished,
And twilight falls upon the mammoth stands.
When a stooper picks a ticket from the fifty-dollar wicket,
And looks upon the dead wealth in his hands.

He'll recall days long ago, when the picture wasn't so
And crowds were small and didn't bet much loot.
When they came from near and far, by buggy, foot and car
To be present on this day of great repute.

He'll see the hats and dresses and the pretty women's tresses,
And gents in tails and top hats by the score.
The odds-men at their work and clods of flying dirt
As the winner gallops home amidst the roar.

And so it is befittin', as another chapter's written
In this classic that has stood the test of time.
That we scribble little notes and perhaps some anecdotes,
Thus the reason for the discourse and the rhyme.

Johnny Needle-Nose

by Jim Coleman

Johnny Needle-Nose braced himself against the wind of the winter night as he entered the foaling barn and closed the door behind him. He stamped the snow from his shoes and looked across into the stall, where the Blow-Back Kid was down on his knees beside the old mare. The kid shook his head soberly and said: "It's no use — the foal was still-born and the mare's a cooked goose. Damn vets never are around when you want 'em. Anyhow, this snow's too deep for travelling, and even the chief croaker at Bellevue could-n't do anything for this old hide. Don't know why you've bothered about her all these years – she never was worth a quarter."

Johnny Needle-Nose didn't answer, but he stared at the wall for a moment, lost in thought. A pail of water was whistling gently on the pot-bellied stove that warmed the little barn. The Blow-Back Kid spat at the stove and wiped his hands on his grim dunga-rees. The spittle disappeared almost instantaneously as it hit the red-hot side of the stove.

"She never was worth a quarter," persisted the Blow-Back Kid. "Damned if I can under-stand how a man can get married to a horse - particularly some old bum that never was worth a quarter."

You find strange people around a racetrack. Good men, bad men and men that are just plain shiftless and lazy. The best thing about racing is the horses, honest, loyal and uncom-plaining. It would be difficult to classify Johnny Needle-Nose, but you couldn't call him a bad man. Sometimes it's wise not to ask too many questions around a racetrack because the yesterdays are nobody's business and it's only an even-money bet that the sun will rise again tomorrow morning. It was nobody's business, for instance, that Johnny Needle-Nose had been an altar boy and had studied for the priesthood. You can't tell who you'll find around a racetrack. The passage of years had left Johnny Needle-Nose's face seamed and scarred and his hair was white and, as far as anyone knew, he had been around horses all his life, and now he had money and good horses, and he sat in the clubhouse while other men mucked out the stalls and walked the hots.

Johnny looked at the Kid and looked down at the old mare and lit another cigaret. As the smoke curled upward Johnny thought of the mare. Her name was Just Julia.

"She's better off dead, anyhow," said Blow-Back. "Too bad the foal didn't live, though. Looked as if he might have been a good little colt. Better than his mammy — bet this old bag of bones never won a race."

"She won one," said Johnny, almost to himself.

There was no point in telling the Kid about it. It was too many years ago - when Jaurez was a roaring border town - and, besides, the Kid wouldn't have understood. Johnny Needle-Nose stood there, while the life ebbed out of the old mare and he was lost until the cigarette burned down to scorch his fingers. Her name was Just Julia and the Blow-Back Kid wouldn't remember it, but she had beaten a horse named The Tuscan. He shook himself as he thought of the years that had passed since then.

He had arrived at Juarez, sleeping in a box-car that carried Just Julia to the track. He slept in a corner of her stall, too - his was a one-horse outfit and they didn't even give him a tackroom. As far as that goes, he didn't need a tackroom, because by that time he didn't have anything to put into it. He didn't have anything in his pockets either, and he stole the feed for her and he galloped her himself on those bleak winter mornings. He was as close to starving as man can be in a land of plenty. He had no friends and no enemies because, even then, Johnny Needle-Nose was a loner.

He had Just Julia because she had broken down as a two-year-old and her owners had given her to the thin-faced, long-nosed kid who asked for her. He had doctored her and babied her, and his loving treatment had restored her to a semblance of the strength and speed which was her birthright.

So, he entered her at Juarez, He couldn't afford to bet on her, and he tightened her saddle girths and gave the boy a leg-up and he crossed his fingers. She was at The Tuscan's throat latch when they turned for home, and in the long, bitter battle down to the wire she ran his eyeballs out. She beat him, but they had to van her off the track and she never ran again.

Johnny Needle-Nose

Johnny Needle-Nose couldn't afford to bet on her, but the purse that she won that day gave him his stake. It was one of those propitious moments that occurs once in the life of every man. From that day he never looked back to the yesterdays.

He looked down at the old mare as she lay there, dying. Her troubled eyes looked back at him, but there was nothing that man could do. Strange, he thought, that horses, infinitely nobler than man, are denied a final hour of dignity in death.

Desperately he thought of something that he might do for her. Suddenly a small bell tinkled distantly in his memory. He thought of a place, far away. He saw men in simple vestments. He heard the chanting of many voices.

He took off his hat and stood erect. Reaching out his foot with the tip of his shoe he knocked the hat from the head of the Blow-Back Kid who was kneeling still beside the old mare.

The long-forgotten Latin words came haltingly to Johnny Needle-Nose's lips at first. Then they poured out of him as if it was only yesterday. He made a sign with his hands. "What does that mean?" said the Blow-Back Kid, his eyes on Johnny Needle-Nose while his hands groped behind him in the straw, searching for his hat.

"Nothing," said Johnny Needle-Nose wearily, "nothing at all."

And, without a backward look, he went away from there.

March 14, 1946
Reprinted with permission from the Globe and Mail

November Song

November month is here again,
It's true, we must admit;
The racing season's growing short
And we don't mind a bit.

We are bedded down at Woodbine,
The track that we call home;
Where soon we'll break the yearlings
And hear the north wind moan.

Perhaps there will be those who'll head
For places south, and sunny.
And some will stay behind to duck
The snowballs (that ain't funny).

But still no matter where we go,
It doesn't matter really,
For April ninth will find us all
Right back at old Fort Erie.

A Finicky Clientele

Glossary

BOWED TENDON:	A thickening of a horse's leg tendon(s) following injury, initially a result of fluid, later a result of scar tissue.
BUG BOY:	An apprentice jockey
BULL RING:	A half-mile track
BLISTER:	A medication used to treat a bowed tendon.
CAPS:	Baby teeth (two-year-olds)
CROSS BAR HOTEL:	Jail
FIGURE-EIGHT:	A piece of leather headgear in the shape of a figure-eight, designed to keep a horse's mouth closed while training or racing.
GIANT OF THE NORTH:	Woodbine Race Track
GYP:	Short for gypsy
GUINEA:	A groom
HOMBERLIE:	A ne'er do well
IRONS:	Stirrups
JIM'S I.C.R.A.	The 'Incorporated Canada Racetrack Association' which laid down the rules of racing in Ontario. It was founded and administered by James Heffering, a prominent Canadian owner and breeder of Thoroughbred race horses. The I.C.R.A. was the forerunner of the present Ontario Racing Commision.
LILY WHITES:	Bandages
MUCKSACK:	A large sheet of burlap made by stitching two large grain sacks together. It is used to carry manure and straw from a horse's stall to a manure box.
ON THE CUFF:	A purchase on credit. Usually one dollar down, with a portion of each future winning purse paid to the original owner until the agreed purchase price is paid in full.
O.R.C.	Ontario Racing Commission
PLATER:	A cheap claiming horse
POT:	Purse money, or purse
POKOLODIE:	The outside rail of a race track
SHAKEDOWN BED:	A straw bed, made by shaking out a few bales of straw on the floor of a box stall and covering the straw with a horse blanket.
SPLINT:	A thickening of soft or bony tissue between the small splint bone and the main leg of the horse, resulting from injury.
STOOPER:	Person who picks up discarded mutuel tickets at the racetrack, hoping to find a winning ticket.
STRING:	A stable of racehorses
THE DUFFERIN: (DUFFERIN PARK)	A half-mile track operated by the Orpen family and located near Bloor and Dufferin streets in Toronto. Thoroughbred and Harness racing was conducted there from 1907 to 1955.
THRUSH:	A disease of the hoof.
TACK:	Saddle, bridle etc.

All of these ballads and poems were written
in the late 1950s and early 1960s
and were published at that time in various publications, including:
The Canadian Horse
The Guineas' Gazette
The Daily Racing Form

Acknowledgements

Jim Bannon
Gerry Belanger
Stan Bergstein
Centrefield Willie (William Burrell)
Louis Cauz
Art Coleman
Margaret Cyr
Tony Demarco
John S. Findley, DVM
Douglas Haig
Sandy Hawley
Ronald C. Johnson
Ronald T. (Ron) Robinson
David A. Stevenson
Curtis Stock
Bill Tallon
Jim Taylor
Daryl Wells Jr.

Jim Coleman

Jim Coleman was introduced to the sport of Thoroughbred racing when he was a youngster. As he grew, his love for the sport did too. He entertained newspaper readers across Canada for years with tales of backstretch characters and the intriguing world of Thoroughbred racing, beginning in 1931, at the *Winnipeg Tribune*.

Coleman enjoyed and glorified the underdog: a racetracker down on his luck; the longshots with the courage to overcome the odds – a 20-to-1 nag; a team down four goals or three touchdowns.

On January 14, 2000, Canada's premier sportswriter died of heart failure at age 89 in a Vancouver hospital. Coleman, who wrote his columns while chomping on a cigar, refused to retire from his job at the *Vancouver Province*. He worked to the end – his last column appeared the day he died.

He was a modest man who had friends in high places and low, and never put himself above or below any of them. He covered every sport imaginable with eloquence, wit and an unfailing love that earned him a position as Canada's first nationally syndicated sports columnist and countless honours, including the Order of Canada as well as induction into five Canadian Sports Halls of Fame.

Author of three books, *A Hoofprint On My Heart, Long Ride On A Hobby Horse* and *Hockey Is Our Game*, Coleman's 70-year writing career enabled him to regale readers of the *Vancouver Province, Edmonton Journal, Edmonton Bulletin, The Canadian Press, The Globe and Mail* and the chain of Southam Newspapers.

He attracted notables and some of lesser reputations. A partial list of his cronies and the characters he brought to life in his columns ranged from The Good Kid, Deacon Jack Allen, Morris Fishman, R. James Speers, Doc Hodgson, Big Jim Fair, Irish Davy, Middle Of The Road Red, Chatahoochee Smith, Michigan Ike, Montreal Red, Whittlin' Knifong, Helen The Booster, Doug Ness, Whittier Park Slim, and High-Ball Kelly. Some weren't associated primarily with horse racing, but they were woven into the rich coulourful fabric of the sport.

In 2005, Vancouver Sports Columnist Jim Taylor assembled some of Coleman's finest pieces in a book called *The Best of Jim Coleman: Fifty Years of Canadian Sport from the man who saw it all*.